Alexander the Great: The Power of Vision is a unique, thought-provoking exploration of one of history's most powerful leaders, Alexander the Great, penned by the esteemed ChatStick Team. Rather than simply recounting the known history, this work delves deeper into the psyche of Alexander, tracing his visionary power that compelled his unparalleled successes. The book transports readers back to Alexander's time, weaving a compelling narrative that seamlessly blends history, psychology, and leadership studies. It represents an original and insightful perspective on Alexander's life, achievements, and enduring influence on world history.

s much an exploration of leadership and ambition as it is a iography, "Alexander the Great: The Power of Vision" is a ust-read for history enthusiasts, leadership scholars, and veryone intrigued by the life of this remarkable king and his nduring legacy.

chatvariety.com

table of contents

chatvariety.com

table of contents

INTRODUCTION

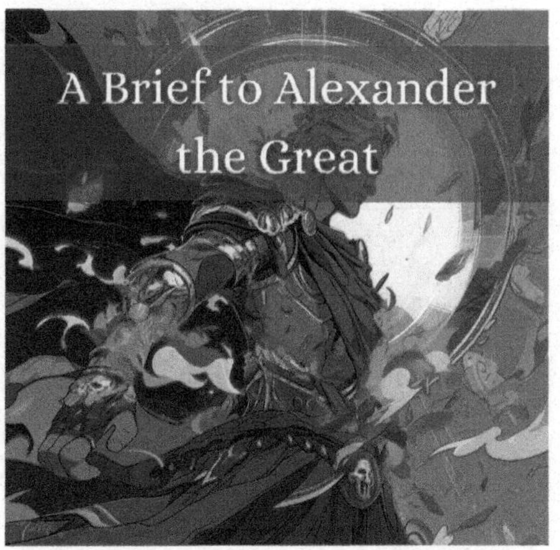

Welcome, dear reader, to an intriguing journey through time, leading us back to the remarkable era of a man whose vision forever shaped the course of human history - Alexander the Great.

Born into a world torn by strife and yearning for unity, Alexander III of Macedon, better known as Alexander the Great, was no ordinary man. He was a prodigious figure whose exploits have inspired, influenced, and at times, intimidated, historians, leaders, and visionaries over the centuries. His life, though brief, was replete with deeds so grand, dreams so ambitious, and a personality so compelling that his story continues to captivate us, even millennia after his demise.

Alexander was born in 356 BC in Pella, the ancient capital of Macedonia. He was the son of King Philip II and Queen Olympias, a fervently spiritual woman who filled young Alexander's mind with tales of heroes and gods, likely sparking his life-long quest for glory. But Alexander's mental acuity and strategic prowess weren't merely a product of his mother's stories. The renowned philosopher Aristotle was his tutor during his formative years, under whose guidance Alexander developed a profound interest in philosophy, sciences, and arts. A prodigy who would later metamorphose into a military genius, Alexander had begun to exhibit signs of his exceptional leadership from an early age.

At the age of 20, in the aftermath of his father's assassination, Alexander ascended the throne. Yet, unlike other young kings, he did not remain ensnared in the comforts of his court. Instead, he embarked on a venture that would become one of the greatest military campaigns in history. From Greece to Egypt and as far east as India, Alexander's ambitious vision led him through a series of relentless conquests. His strategic genius in battle, coupled with his diplomatic finesse and his respect for different cultures, was instrumental in creating an empire that, at its zenith, stretched over three continents.

Yet, Alexander's vision extended beyond military conquests. He dreamt of a world united under a single banner, where cultural and intellectual exchanges would be the norm rather than the exception. Alexander's belief in this vision was so resolute that he encouraged intermarriages between his soldiers and the women of the conquered lands, himself taking several foreign wives. His effort to blend diverse cultures was one of the early instances of globalisation, leading to what we now refer to as the Hellenistic period.

However, the life of this remarkable visionary, who marched tirelessly toward his dreams, was cut short. Alexander died in 323 BC in Babylon at the young age of 32, leaving behind a legacy as vast and enduring as the empire he built. The empire, bereft of its visionary leader, crumbled into fragments, but the impact of Alexander's vision transcended the confines of his empire. It catalyzed cultural syntheses across these fragments, left an indelible imprint on the annals of military strategy, and set an example for visionary leadership that continues to inspire leaders across various fields.

As we delve into the subsequent chapters, we'll explore how Alexander's vision took root, how it guided his actions and decisions, and how it has continued to reverberate throughout history. We hope this journey not only enlightens you about this extraordinary historical figure but also stirs you to reflect upon the power of vision in our own lives. After all, as Alexander the Great showed us, a man with a vision can indeed change the world. Let's begin this fascinating expedition into the past, into the life of Alexander - a king, a warrior, a visionary.

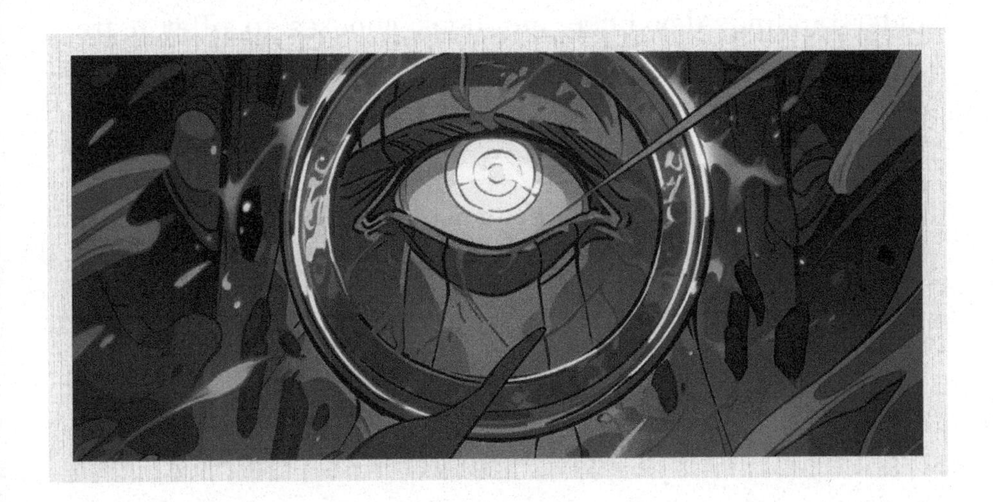

Before we embark on our odyssey into the life of Alexander the Great, let's take a moment to illuminate the unique prism through which we'll be exploring his tale - the lens of his visionary power.

Countless volumes have been penned about Alexander the Great, some focusing on his military strategies, others delving into the breadth of his empire, and still more analyzing his leadership style. While these dimensions are indeed crucial to understanding Alexander, our book chooses to offer a fresh perspective - we will journey through his life, not just as a king or a conqueror, but as a visionary.

So, what is this visionary power we speak of, and why is it so important in understanding Alexander the Great?

A visionary is one who can imagine a future that is not only different from the present but also far superior. They possess an unusual capacity for foresight, a rare ability to visualize possibilities beyond the immediate, and the resilience to turn their dreams into reality. Visionaries, in essence, are dreamers with the tenacity to manifest their dreams. They inspire change, drive progress, and transform the world around them. And Alexander, with his unparalleled ambitions, undaunted spirit, and the empire he forged, exemplifies this visionary ethos.

Alexander's vision was far from ordinary. It encompassed not just territorial expansion but also the fusion of diverse cultures. He envisioned a world that was not fragmented by parochial boundaries but united under shared knowledge and mutual respect. His dream was an empire where Greek philosophy coexisted with Persian art, where Macedonian soldiers married Bactrian women, and where wisdom from India was revered as much as Athenian literature. This vision for a cosmopolitan empire was a testament to Alexander's broad-mindedness and his intrinsic understanding of the power of cultural amalgamation.

The extraordinary resilience with which Alexander pursued this vision also marks his visionary prowess. Despite facing resistance, setbacks, and even potential mutiny, Alexander never lost sight of his vision. He ventured into unknown territories, confronted formidable armies, and endured physical hardships, all driven by the compelling force of his vision.

However, as we explore the power of Alexander's vision, we must also examine its inherent contradictions and the shadows it cast. How did Alexander reconcile his ambition for a united world with the devastation caused by his campaigns? How did his vision for cultural integration sit alongside his often authoritarian rule? Our exploration of Alexander's visionary power will not shy away from these paradoxes. On the contrary, it will delve into them, seeking to understand the man behind the legend in all his complexity.

As we traverse through the chapters, each will illuminate a different facet of Alexander's vision, from its seeds in his childhood to its impact on his military strategies, from its influence on his perception of divinity to its culmination in his dream for a unified world.

By focusing on Alexander's visionary power, we hope to offer a fresh perspective on his life, one that recognizes him not just as a formidable king or a strategic genius, but as a man with the power to dream, the courage to chase those dreams, and the tenacity to make them come true. So, let's begin our journey into the visionary world of Alexander the Great. A fascinating expedition awaits us!

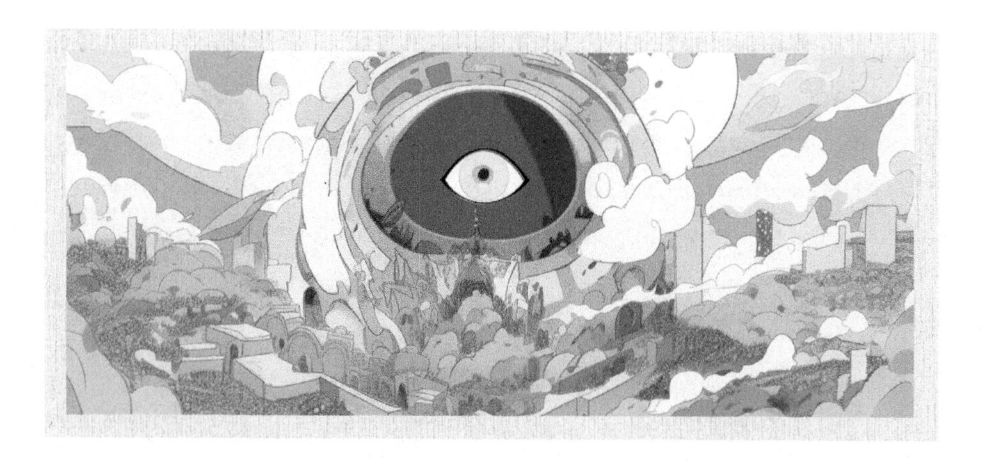

THE SEED OF VISION

Before we delve into the extraordinary life of Alexander the Great, it is crucial to understand the world that birthed and shaped him - the kingdom of Macedonia during his early years. The environment in which Alexander grew up played a substantial role in molding his perspectives, values, and ultimately, his visionary power.

In the late 4th century BCE, Macedonia was a rising power on the fringes of the classical Greek world. Under the rule of King Philip II, Alexander's father, Macedonia transformed from a turbulent, divided kingdom into a consolidated powerhouse.

King Philip II was a transformative figure. He reorganized the Macedonian army, introducing innovative strategies, and building a force that was the envy of many Greek city-states. Under his rule, Macedonia not only increased in military power but also became politically unified and economically robust. This was the stage onto which Alexander was born, a stage that presented him with a model of leadership and the possibility of greatness.

Yet, Macedonia was also seen as a cultural backwater by the sophisticated city-states of southern Greece, like Athens and Sparta. Despite being Greek-speaking, the Macedonians were often looked down upon for their 'barbaric' lifestyle, their monarchical government as opposed to the democracy or oligarchy preferred by many Greek city-states, and their rustic manners. This sense of being an outsider, of being 'othered' despite shared ancestry, possibly had a profound impact on young Alexander, fueling his ambition to not just be a part of the Hellenic world, but to dominate it and further, to create a cultural blend that transcended the narrow definitions of 'civilized' and 'barbaric.'

Alexander's early years in Macedonia were also marked by the influence of strong personalities. His father, Philip, was a towering figure, a shrewd diplomat, and a military genius who provided a practical model of leadership. His mother, Olympias, a woman of high spirit and profound religious fervor, instilled in him a belief in his own divine destiny. These influences, combined with the unique cultural and political position of Macedonia, likely played a significant role in shaping Alexander's vision.

Moreover, Macedonia's geographical position, nestled between the classical Greek world to the south, the Thracians and Illyrians to the north, the Persians to the east, and with connections to Italy and Carthage to the west, offered Alexander a broad perspective on the diversity of cultures, customs, and peoples. This was a world full of possibilities, a world that could be unified, and Alexander, from a young age, seemed to have perceived this potential.

In the kingdom of Macedonia, the seeds of ambition, desire for greatness, cultural blending, and universal rule were sowed in the mind of young Alexander. This formative landscape was instrumental in shaping the vision that would guide Alexander's path. As we move forward, we will delve deeper into these early influences, examining how they guided and formed the visionary power of Alexander the Great. Our journey is just beginning, and there's much more to discover. Let's venture forth into the life of one of history's greatest visionaries.

Following our exploration of the Macedonian world that formed the backdrop of Alexander's life, let's delve into the very beginning of his story: his birth and the legends that envelop it. Just like the man himself, the circumstances of Alexander's birth were anything but ordinary, already steeped in tales that evoked grandeur and divinity, which would later shape his vision and ambitions.

Alexander III, later known as Alexander the Great, was born in Pella, the ancient capital of Macedonia, in 356 BCE. His parents were King Philip II and his wife, Olympias, an Epirote princess. The birth of a royal heir was always a significant event, but Alexander's birth was accompanied by omens and legends that elevated the occasion to mythic proportions.

The most frequently recounted tale involves a series of prodigious events occurring on the night of Alexander's birth. On this fateful night, it is said, the Temple of Artemis at Ephesus, one of the Seven Wonders of the Ancient World, burned down. The destruction of such an iconic structure was seen as an omen of a significant event. When the temple's priests proclaimed that the fire was a portent signaling the birth of one who would conquer the world, it only added to the grandeur surrounding Alexander's entrance into the world.

In addition to this, there were legends related by Alexander's mother herself. Olympias was known to be a devout follower of the snake-worshipping cult of Dionysus. She claimed that on the eve of her wedding, she dreamt of a thunderbolt striking her womb, from which a great fire sprang up that spread far and wide before extinguishing. This dream was later interpreted by the seers as a sign that her son would be a heroic figure whose fame would reach beyond the limits of the mortal world.

Another tale Olympias often shared was about a snake seen lying beside her while she was still carrying Alexander. This snake, the ancient symbol of the earth deity, was interpreted as the god Zeus himself. The implication that Alexander was the son of Zeus was a recurring theme in his life and would greatly impact his sense of self and destiny.

King Philip, too, had visions concerning his son. In one, it was said that he sealed Olympias's womb with the symbol of a lion during her pregnancy, which the court seers prophesied as indicating that Alexander would be as brave and dominant as a lion. In another, he saw himself inscribing the symbol of the universe onto Olympias's womb, hinting at the world-conquering destiny of his unborn son.

Of course, it's crucial to remember that these stories have been handed down through generations, each adding its touch of embroidery. However, what is clear is that from the beginning of his life, Alexander was wrapped in the cloak of divinity and greatness. His extraordinary birth stories set him apart, nurturing the seed of a unique vision in his heart. This perception of himself as not just a prince, but as a figure of destiny, undoubtedly played a part in shaping the audacious vision that would drive him to unimaginable heights.

In our next exploration, we'll venture into the hallowed halls of Alexander's education, where the seed of vision planted at his birth began to germinate under the guidance of one of history's greatest philosophers. The journey of Alexander's life is a thrilling saga, and we're only just getting started.

Let's now turn our attention to the young Alexander and his formative years, where the seed of his visionary future continued to germinate. Alexander's education, as you'll see, was no ordinary upbringing. It was a stage for shaping one of the greatest conquerors the world has ever seen.

In his early years, Alexander received his education at the royal court of Macedonia, where his first tutor, Leonidas, a relative of his mother, laid the foundation of his early learning. Under Leonidas, Alexander received a strict military upbringing, learning the arts of warfare and kingship. However, Leonidas also introduced Alexander to a passion that would remain with him throughout his life - the love for the works of Homer, especially the Iliad. Alexander would sleep with a copy of it under his pillow, drawing inspiration from the heroics of Achilles.

Alexander's true intellectual and visionary awakening, however, would come from his next tutor, a man who needs no introduction - Aristotle. When Alexander was 13 years old, his father, King Philip, recognizing the unique capabilities of his son, hired Aristotle, one of the most acclaimed philosophers of the time, to educate him. The School of Mieza, a temple close to the Macedonian capital of Pella, became Alexander's classroom.

Under Aristotle's guidance, Alexander studied a wide range of subjects including science, geography, zoology, and medicine. However, it was Aristotle's teachings on philosophy, ethics, and politics that had the most profound impact on Alexander's mindset. The young prince was not just learning facts and skills; he was learning how to think, how to lead, and how to envision a better world. It was Aristotle who instilled in Alexander the belief that a great leader must be a great learner first.

Moreover, it was during these formative years that Alexander met a group of boys of similar age, who would become his lifelong friends and trusted companions on his future campaigns. Among them were Hephaestion, who would become his closest confidant, and Ptolemy, who would later become a Pharaoh of Egypt. These relationships were also a crucial part of Alexander's education, teaching him the values of friendship, loyalty, and teamwork.

What sets Alexander's education apart is the holistic approach that was taken. He was not only being groomed to be a king who could command armies but also a leader with a vision who could win hearts. He was learning how to be strong and compassionate, how to be a warrior and a scholar, how to command respect, and give it in return.

While his education under Aristotle ended when he was 16, the teachings and lessons he received stayed with him. As we will see in the chapters to come, Alexander's education was instrumental in forming his grand vision of a united world. His keen intellect, his unquenchable curiosity about the world, his strategic and tactical genius, his leadership style, and his respect for different cultures can all be traced back to these crucial formative years.

In our next journey, we will witness how Alexander's visions began to take shape when he ascended the throne of Macedonia. It's here that we'll start seeing the sprouts of the seed of vision that was planted at his birth and nurtured during his formative years. So, let's continue our journey into the extraordinary life of Alexander the Great.

As we've seen, Alexander was not only born in unique circumstances but also received an exceptional education. However, it was under the influence of Aristotle, the philosopher extraordinaire, that his perspective widened, and his early visions started to form. Aristotle's teachings had an indelible impact on the young prince's mind, shaping him into a visionary who would later change the course of history.

When Aristotle first met Alexander, he was a bright but raw diamond, in desperate need of a skilled artisan. The philosopher saw potential in Alexander, a kindred spirit driven by curiosity and thirst for knowledge. Recognizing this potential, Aristotle took it upon himself to mold the young prince into a true leader, capable of harnessing his remarkable talents and ambitions for the greater good of mankind.

The philosophical framework provided by Aristotle was instrumental in shaping Alexander's worldview. Aristotle believed in the concept of "eudaimonia," often translated as "happiness" or "flourishing," which could only be achieved through virtue. These teachings deeply influenced Alexander's vision of leadership. The lessons he learned about virtue, justice, and wisdom became the cornerstones of his ethical understanding and his approach to leadership.

Aristotle also taught Alexander about political science, emphasizing the importance of a leader's duty to his citizens and the need for unity and harmony within a state. These teachings sparked Alexander's grand vision of a unified empire where diverse cultures could coexist in harmony, an idea far ahead of his time.

Interestingly, it was Aristotle's teachings on natural science that perhaps had the most profound impact on Alexander's visions. By learning about the vastness and diversity of the natural world, Alexander developed a desire to explore, understand, and unite the world under one banner. It's no coincidence that Alexander's empire stretched across three continents, reflecting his aspiration to understand and harmonize the diversity of the world.

However, it's important to note that while Aristotle was the sculptor shaping the stone, Alexander was not a passive recipient. He actively engaged with Aristotle's teachings, questioned them, and adapted them to his own understanding. The molding process was very much a two-way interaction. It's this active engagement with his education that allowed Alexander to internalize these lessons, which would later manifest in his visionary leadership.

Let's not forget the role Aristotle played in shaping Alexander's love for literature and arts. The appreciation for the arts was a key element of Aristotle's educational curriculum, and Alexander embraced it with open arms. The Iliad, in particular, held a special place in Alexander's heart, as he identified with its hero, Achilles. This deep love for literature and arts would later influence Alexander's vision for a culturally rich and diverse empire.

In short, the time Alexander spent under Aristotle's tutelage was transformative. The philosophical, ethical, and political teachings he received helped mold his early visions of a unified, diverse empire, promoting peace, cultural exchange, and mutual respect. In our following chapters, we will see how these early visions, shaped under Aristotle's guidance, guided Alexander's actions as he ascended the throne and embarked on his world-conquering journey.

We must remember, though, that while Aristotle provided the initial mold, it was Alexander's own extraordinary qualities – his unwavering determination, his thirst for knowledge, his boldness, and his ability to inspire others – that allowed him to transform these early visions into reality. As we journey further into Alexander's life, we will see these qualities in action, illuminating the path to his enduring legacy.

THE THRONE AND A VISION

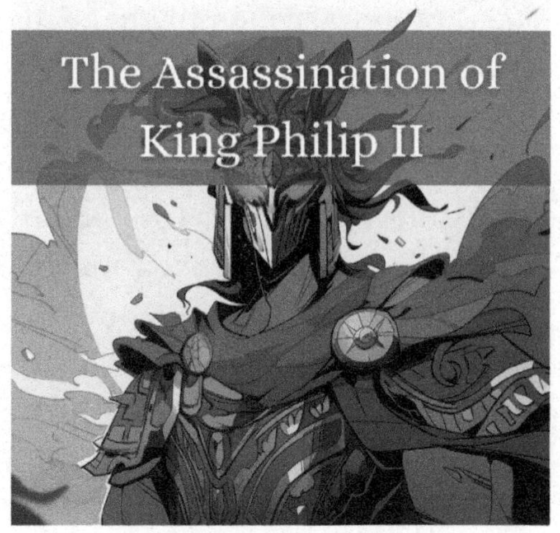

As we delve into this chapter, we come across a critical point in Alexander's life, a moment when destiny came knocking at his door - the assassination of King Philip II. While it was a tragic event, it thrust Alexander onto the stage of history with a grand vision for his people.

King Philip II was a remarkable ruler who transformed Macedonia from a troubled region on the fringes of the Greek world into a dominant military power. His assassination in 336 BC shocked Macedonia and the Greek states under his sway. However, it's the circumstances around this event, and its subsequent impact on Alexander's vision, that makes it noteworthy.

Philip was murdered by one of his bodyguards, Pausanias, at a public event, a wedding feast. The reasons behind the assassination are entangled in a web of personal grudges, political intrigue, and possibly, foreign involvement. However, for our young prince, now turned king, the reasons mattered less than the reality of the situation – his father was dead, and he had a kingdom to rule.

The throne wasn't simply handed over to Alexander, though. He had to secure his position amidst internal opposition and external threats. The very skills he had honed under Aristotle's tutelage came into play, as he used his intellect, persuasive ability, and the respect he commanded among the military to secure his position as the King of Macedonia.

With the throne now under his control, Alexander didn't waste time mourning. He realized the precarious situation his kingdom was in. With Philip's death, many of the Greek states saw an opportunity to break free from Macedonian rule. There was an urgent need for stability, unity, and a firm hand to guide the kingdom.

It was in these circumstances that Alexander's vision began to evolve. His immediate vision was clear - to establish his authority and keep the unity of Greece intact. He knew he had to follow in his father's footsteps, but he also understood that he had to create his own path, his own vision, for the sake of Macedonia and Greece.

Alexander's vision wasn't limited to maintaining the status quo; it was far more ambitious. His vision included transforming Macedonia into a power that would not just dominate the Greek world but also stand against the mighty Persian Empire. As Aristotle's pupil, he had an extensive understanding of Persia's wealth, power, and cultural heritage. He realized that the unity and prosperity of his own kingdom could be ensured only by projecting power beyond its borders.

In essence, the assassination of King Philip II and Alexander's ascension to the throne was a crucial turning point. It was a moment when Alexander's visions, shaped during his early years under Aristotle, started taking a more definite form, influenced by the demands of his newfound role. As we will see in the following chapters, these visions were not mere fantasies but powerful drivers of action that would lead Alexander to make his indelible mark on history.

But for now, let us hold our horses and not gallop too far ahead. In the next section, we will look at how Alexander ascended to the throne and his immediate vision for a unified Greece - a vision that would soon stretch far beyond the Greek city-states, towards the horizons that even his ambitious father would not have dared to gaze upon. As we traverse through these formative years of his reign, we'll discover how the seed of his vision, planted and nurtured under Aristotle's guidance, started to bloom under the Macedonian sun.

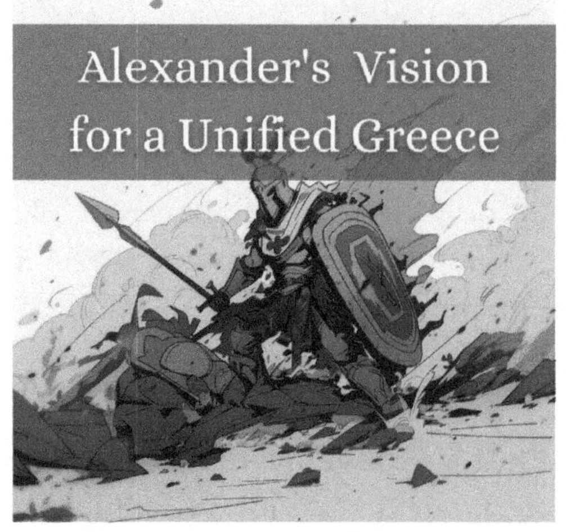

In the wake of the shocking assassination of King Philip II, the throne of Macedonia stood vacant, not yet cold, awaiting the successor. This successor, the torchbearer of Philip's legacy, was his son, Alexander III. In the previous section, we examined the circumstances surrounding the assassination. Now, we'll venture into the fascinating tale of Alexander's ascension and his immediate vision for a unified Greece.

Alexander, only twenty years old at the time, wasted no time in securing his position. He quickly quelled the immediate threats to his throne from potential rivals, including his cousin Amyntas and two Macedonian princes, using a mix of diplomatic finesse and military might.

The Greek city-states, seeing the death of Philip II as a chance to regain their freedom, began to stir with the hopes of rebellion. The Thebans and Athenians, in particular, had grown tired of Macedonian dominance and sought to exploit this moment of perceived weakness. But they were to discover that the new king was as formidable as his father, if not more.

Alexander, schooled by the great Aristotle and mentored by his father, had been instilled with a deep understanding of both Greek philosophy and military tactics. This background allowed him to apply a unique blend of intellectual acuity, strategic thinking, and raw physical power.

His vision for Greece wasn't just about maintaining the status quo; it was much more ambitious. He sought to unify the Greek city-states under one banner, not through oppression or tyranny, but with the vision of a common identity and purpose. He saw a unified Greece as a significant power, one that could rival the mighty Persian Empire, extending its influence beyond the Aegean and transforming the known world.

Alexander knew that to make this vision a reality, he needed to ensure stability at home. Hence, he turned his attention to the simmering dissent in the Greek city-states. Displaying remarkable political shrewdness and military brilliance, he launched expeditions to suppress the revolts, managing to put down the rebellion and secure the allegiance of the Greek states in less than two years.

He made a powerful statement by showing mercy to the Athenians, a decision that won him their reluctant respect. But he also demonstrated his ruthlessness when he destroyed Thebes, making it a horrifying example of the fate awaiting those who defied his rule.

Alexander's decisions were not driven merely by the pursuit of power. They were guided by his vision of a Pan-Hellenic empire, an empire where the Greek city-states were not vassals, but partners, sharing common objectives and values. His vision included the amalgamation of cultures and knowledge, the spread of Hellenism, and the promotion of science and philosophy.

In essence, Alexander's ascension to the throne and his vision for a unified Greece were instrumental in setting the stage for the epochal events that would soon unfold. As we will explore in the next chapters, his visions went far beyond the borders of Macedonia and Greece, reaching out to touch Asia and Africa. His dreams didn't just dwell in the realms of imagination, but were given life and form, influencing the course of history in a profound way.

In the next chapter, we will travel with Alexander as he embarks on his grand Pan-Hellenic campaign against Persia, a pivotal moment that would truly test the power and reach of his vision. Together, we will discover how this young king, imbued with the courage of a lion and the wisdom of a philosopher, embarks on a journey to turn his dream of a unified empire into a reality. For now, let us revel in the awe-inspiring tale of a young king, barely out of his teens, who dared to dream not just for himself, but for an entire civilization.

A VISION BEYOND HORIZONS

As we turn the pages from Alexander's ascension and the unification of Greece, we find ourselves drawn into the most significant phase of his reign - the Pan-Hellenic campaign against Persia. Alexander's grand vision was about to be put to the test on a scale never seen before.

It's important to understand that this wasn't merely a military campaign fuelled by a young king's ambitions. Rather, it was a quest to actualize a dream that had begun to take shape in Alexander's mind as he sat at the feet of Aristotle in Mieza. The Persian Empire, formidable and seemingly unassailable, was not merely a rival to be defeated. It was a challenge that called for Alexander's grand vision of unification and harmony.

At the heart of this vision was the idea of Pan-Hellenism, a union of Greek city-states. Alexander's father, Philip II, had already laid some of the groundwork for this vision by forming the League of Corinth and setting the stage for a united front against Persia. However, with Philip's assassination, Alexander had to take the reins of this unfinished plan.

The challenge was immense. Persia was an established empire with vast resources at its disposal. Its armies outnumbered the Macedonian forces and its wealth was legendary. Yet, the young Macedonian king was not deterred. With his innate strategic acumen, indomitable spirit, and the backing of united Greek city-states, he prepared to take on the Persian giant.

To understand the magnitude of this undertaking, it's worth remembering that this was not just a military expedition. This was a cultural quest, an effort to bring together the East and the West. It was a vision that Alexander believed would lead to a greater understanding and exchange of ideas, just as his tutor Aristotle had once emphasized the importance of shared knowledge.

But, as we know, grand visions require grand actions. And so, in 334 BC, Alexander led his forces across the Hellespont, the narrow strait that served as the boundary between Europe and Asia. This marked the beginning of his legendary campaign against Persia, a journey that would take him through Asia Minor, Syria, Egypt, Mesopotamia, and beyond.

It's crucial to appreciate that Alexander was not merely a conqueror. He was a visionary leader who, even amidst the chaos of war, never lost sight of his larger goal. He did not seek to merely defeat Persia, but rather to bring together two distinct cultures and create a new world where ideas, traditions, and knowledge could freely flow.

From this point onward, Alexander's vision was set on the horizon, a horizon that extended far beyond the confines of Greece and Macedonia. He dared to imagine a world larger than anything known to his contemporaries, a world in which Greek culture and Persian heritage intertwined, fostering an era of enlightenment and progress.

In the chapters to come, we will journey alongside Alexander as he breathes life into this vision. We will witness his triumphs and tribulations, his courage and charisma, his visionary leadership and, inevitably, his human flaws.

For now, let's reflect on the commencement of this Pan-Hellenic campaign against Persia, an expedition that wasn't just about territorial conquest, but a testament to the power of vision, courage, and unity. A campaign that would see Alexander not only as a great conqueror but also as a leader with a vision beyond horizons.

The name Alexander is synonymous with some of the greatest battles in the annals of human history. However, these weren't mere exhibitions of brute force or tactical supremacy. These battles were an extension of Alexander's grand vision, manifesting on the battlefield through strategic brilliance and charismatic leadership. Among these legendary conflicts, the Battles of Granicus and Issus hold a distinct place. They not only laid the foundation for Alexander's impending conquests but were also a testament to his innovative leadership.

The Battle of Granicus, fought in 334 BC, marked Alexander's first major encounter with the Persian army. His troops were vastly outnumbered, and he faced a formidable enemy on their own territory. The odds were stacked against him, but Alexander, with his vision set firmly on his goals, refused to be swayed.

Alexander's approach to the battle was unconventional. Unlike traditional warfare strategies that prescribed caution when facing superior numbers, Alexander chose to lead a direct charge against the Persian line. His audacious decision was driven not by overconfidence, but by a deep understanding of his own men and their capability. He believed in his men as much as they believed in his vision.

His intuition proved correct. The Macedonians, with Alexander leading the charge, broke through the Persian front, causing a route that resulted in a significant victory for the Greeks. This triumph didn't merely serve as a military success; it was an affirmation of Alexander's vision, a testament to the power of belief, and the undeniable impact of visionary leadership.

Following the victory at Granicus, Alexander's forces pushed further into Persian territory, leading to the decisive Battle of Issus in 333 BC. The circumstances were even more challenging this time. The Persian King Darius III himself commanded the Persian army, which vastly outnumbered Alexander's forces.

Alexander, however, was undeterred. His visionary leadership again came to the fore. He understood the importance of morale and the power of belief. He led from the front, rallying his troops with passionate speeches, reminding them of their shared vision, the unity of Greece, and the glory that awaited them.

In the face of overwhelming odds, Alexander's army held firm, pushing back wave after wave of Persian assaults. The key to this victory was Alexander's use of innovative strategies, including the effective use of the phalanx formation and his expert cavalry tactics. Eventually, the Persian lines crumbled, and King Darius fled, marking another significant victory for Alexander.

The Battles of Granicus and Issus weren't just about military conquests; they were reflections of Alexander's visionary leadership. They showcased the power of a unified vision, the strength of belief, and the potential of well-orchestrated strategies.

These battles signified more than mere territorial gains. They laid the foundation for the coming age of Hellenistic culture, an era marked by the blend of Greek and Eastern influences. They underscored the power of Alexander's vision, a vision not limited to the battlefield but extended to cultural integration, respect for diversity, and the forging of a united empire.

In the next sections, we will explore how Alexander's visionary leadership unfolded beyond the battlefield, guiding him through cultural assimilation, the embrace of divinity, and even the limits of his ambition. But for now, let us appreciate the battles of Granicus and Issus as true examples of Alexander's grand vision and his extraordinary ability to bring that vision to life against the most formidable odds.

Victorious on the battlefield, Alexander was now poised to demonstrate a different facet of his vision. It wasn't merely about conquering foreign lands and expanding his domain but assimilating the best of these foreign cultures and fostering a unified empire.

Alexander's vision for a united empire had an underpinning in his upbringing and education. Having studied under Aristotle, he learned about diverse cultures and the value of harmony among different societies. This vision propelled him to integrate the cultures of the conquered territories rather than merely imposing the Macedonian way of life. He believed that the amalgamation of cultures would create a richer, more vibrant society, thereby fostering unity and peace.

Nowhere was this clearer than in Persia. After the decisive Battle of Issus, Alexander didn't merely install Greek governors and enforce Macedonian laws. Instead, he adopted the Persian administrative system, a tried and tested framework that had governed a vast empire for centuries. This was a radical move, unheard of among most conquerors who would often seek to completely obliterate the existing system and replace it with their own.

But Alexander's vision went further. He didn't just adopt Persian administrative practices; he embraced Persian culture, even adopting Persian dress for himself and encouraging his men to do the same. This decision was met with resistance from his men, who saw it as a betrayal of their own culture. However, for Alexander, it was a tangible way to blend cultures, to bridge the gap between the conquerors and the conquered, to foster mutual respect and understanding.

He promoted intermarriages between his Macedonian soldiers and Persian women, a strategy aimed at solidifying the unity between the two cultures. Alexander himself married the Persian princess Roxana, signaling his personal commitment to this cultural amalgamation.

His approach towards the conquered territories was not limited to Persia. In Egypt, he embraced the local customs and even accepted the title of Pharaoh. By doing so, he presented himself not as a foreign ruler but as a rightful king respecting and upholding local traditions.

This ethos of cultural amalgamation also extended to his army. Alexander's forces, initially purely Macedonian, evolved into a multicultural military powerhouse. Soldiers from conquered territories, including Persians, Egyptians, and later, Indians, were integrated into his army. This allowed him to field a military force that was not just physically robust, but culturally diverse, bringing together the strengths of various cultures under one banner.

Alexander's vision for a united empire was grand and unique for its time. His strategy of cultural integration signified a profound understanding of humanity's interconnectedness. It was a bold experiment in creating a multicultural society, a testament to the power of his vision. His actions underscored a crucial fact that the might of an empire lies not just in its military prowess, but also in the unity and harmony of its people, regardless of their cultural backgrounds.

In this sense, Alexander was not just a military conqueror but a visionary social architect. His vision of a united empire set a precedent for future leaders, showing them the power of cultural assimilation and the importance of unity in diversity.

As we delve deeper into Alexander's journey in subsequent chapters, we will see how this vision influenced his actions, leading to iconic moments like his coronation as Pharaoh and his ambitious campaigns in India. But for now, let us appreciate the audacity of his vision for a united empire, a vision that transcended the norms of his time, showcasing the full power of visionary leadership.

THE PHARAOH'S DIADEM AND ALEXANDER'S DIVINE VISION

After Alexander's successful campaigns in Persia, he turned his gaze towards Egypt, a civilization with a grand history and rich culture. It was here that he would take on a new title, extending his vision from a temporal conqueror to a divine ruler.

The conquest of Egypt was relatively straightforward, primarily because of the Persians' dwindling influence in the region. Egypt had been under Persian rule for nearly two centuries, and there was widespread discontent among the Egyptian population. Therefore, Alexander's arrival was seen not so much as an invasion, but more of a liberation. The Egyptians welcomed Alexander with open arms, eager to be freed from the Persians. This easy transition of power was a testament to Alexander's reputation as a liberator, a facet of his vision that served him well throughout his campaigns.

Once in control, Alexander respected Egyptian culture, continuing his vision of embracing and integrating foreign cultures. This was particularly evident when he made a demanding journey to the Oracle of Ammon in the Siwa Oasis. The oracle was of immense significance to the Egyptians, and by visiting it, Alexander demonstrated his respect for their beliefs. During this visit, the priests of Ammon reportedly addressed Alexander as the son of Zeus-Ammon, acknowledging him as a divine entity. This event marked the genesis of Alexander's divine vision.

Emboldened by the acknowledgment from the Oracle, Alexander took the monumental step of crowning himself as Pharaoh, the living god-king of the Egyptians. This wasn't just a power move; it was a radical integration of the Macedonian king into the religious fabric of Egypt. Alexander the Great, the visionary leader from Macedonia, was now Alexander the Pharaoh, a divine ruler in the eyes of his Egyptian subjects.

By accepting the Pharaoh's diadem, Alexander entered a new phase in his vision - he wasn't just content being a temporal ruler; he aimed to be a divine figure. He understood that to the Egyptians, their Pharaoh was not just a political leader but a religious figurehead. He embodied the gods' will on Earth, providing spiritual guidance along with temporal governance.

This move also made strategic sense. As Pharaoh, Alexander could command greater authority and loyalty from his subjects. More importantly, it allowed him to unify his empire under a dual Macedonian-Egyptian identity. He was the King of Macedonia and the Pharaoh of Egypt, thereby drawing a symbolic bridge between the two cultures.

During his reign as Pharaoh, Alexander funded the construction of many cities, the most famous of which bore his name - Alexandria. The city was envisioned as a cultural and intellectual hub, embodying Alexander's vision of a united empire where knowledge, culture, and commerce flowed freely. Alexandria later went on to become one of the most important cities in the Hellenistic world, a testament to Alexander's far-reaching vision.

The chapter of Egypt in Alexander's life wasn't just about adding another jewel to his crown. It marked the evolution of Alexander's vision from a unified empire towards a more profound, divine connotation. Alexander, the student of Aristotle, the King of Macedonia, and the conqueror of Persia, was now Alexander, the Pharaoh of Egypt, a god-king in the eyes of his subjects. This new divine vision would significantly impact his later campaigns and how he perceived himself, underscoring once again the extraordinary power of his vision.

Once Alexander assumed the role of Pharaoh in Egypt, his self-perception and his vision for the future took a profound turn. His leadership was not only about creating an empire or unifying different cultures; it began to carry a divine, otherworldly characteristic. The chapter of divinity and godhood is a fascinating part of Alexander's life, laden with profound psychological and spiritual aspects.

Being declared as the son of Zeus-Ammon by the priests of the Oracle in Siwa significantly influenced Alexander's understanding of his destiny. This wasn't just a routine political maneuver - Alexander genuinely began to see himself as a divine figure, a manifestation of godly will on Earth. This divine vision of himself played a massive role in shaping his strategies, leadership style, and the decisions he made subsequently.

Alexander's association with godhood was also a pivotal part of his vision for his empire. He wasn't content with the idea of being a mortal king ruling over a physical domain; he saw himself as a divine leader whose realm transcended the mortal world. He integrated the idea of his divinity into his persona and style of rule, utilizing it as a powerful tool to inspire awe and loyalty among his subjects.

This divine vision extended into his military campaigns as well. The famous incident where Alexander sliced the Gordian Knot is a prime example. The knot, according to prophecy, could only be undone by the future ruler of Asia. Alexander, instead of attempting to untie the knot conventionally, sliced it in half with his sword, declaring that it made no difference how the knot was undone. This act wasn't just a display of bravado, but a symbolic assertion of his divine authority and destiny to rule.

Another manifestation of Alexander's association with divinity was his practice of proskynesis, a Persian court custom involving a ceremonial bow that implied a hierarchy between mortals and a god-king. Although this act created friction among his Greek and Macedonian followers, who saw it as a breach of their customs, Alexander insisted upon its practice. By doing so, he further reinforced the divine aspect of his vision and his role as a god-king.

Alexander also consciously used his perceived divinity to his advantage in dealing with conquered people. His divine status was projected and emphasized, instilling both fear and reverence among his subjects. This strategic use of his 'godhood' acted as a unifying force in his multi-ethnic empire, as it was customary across various cultures to see kings as divine or semi-divine entities.

The chapter of Alexander's life dealing with his divinity and association with godhood provides us with a fascinating insight into his mind. It illustrates how his visionary leadership evolved over time and under different influences, eventually incorporating divine elements. The divine aspect of Alexander's vision deeply influenced his leadership style, his handling of conquered populations, and his self-perception. It underscores the fact that Alexander's vision was not stagnant; instead, it was dynamic, adapting, and evolving according to his circumstances and aspirations.

The notion of Alexander's divinity has elicited much debate among historians. Still, irrespective of its validity, it was an integral part of his life and vision. This divine vision made him a figure larger than life, inspiring awe and devotion among his followers while striking fear into his adversaries' hearts. As controversial as it might be, this chapter reiterates the profound and far-reaching impact of Alexander's vision on his path to becoming one of the most iconic figures in world history.

THE POWER OF VISION IN BATTLE

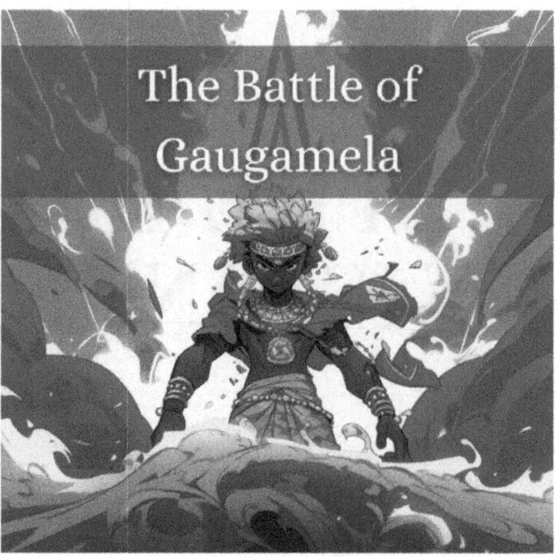

We've covered a lot of ground in our journey through Alexander's life. We've seen him grow from a precocious young prince, to a king, to a living deity in the eyes of his followers. But the heart of Alexander's legend has always been his military genius and unparalleled prowess in battle. The Battle of Gaugamela is where these traits shone most brightly, a testament to Alexander's grand vision and tactical ingenuity. So, buckle up, dear reader, as we delve into the dusty and adrenaline-filled spectacle of this historic encounter.

The Battle of Gaugamela, fought in 331 BC, stands out among Alexander's many victories for its sheer scale and the innovative strategies employed. Alexander, with an army roughly 47,000 strong, faced Darius III, the Persian King, who commanded an estimated force of over 100,000, some accounts even place it closer to a million. The odds were undeniably against the Macedonians.

However, Alexander was not a man easily daunted. His vision for victory was unwavering, even in the face of such staggering odds. He knew that the key to winning this battle was not to match the Persians soldier for soldier, but to outmaneuver them with superior tactics.

One of Alexander's innovative strategies in this battle was his use of the echelon formation, with his troops positioned at an oblique angle rather than in a straight line. This formation served two main purposes. Firstly, it allowed his forces to avoid direct engagement with the full might of the Persian army. Secondly, it drew Darius's forces out of their solid line formation, creating vulnerable gaps.

The Persian King, eager to crush Alexander, took the bait and moved his heavy chariots and cavalry away from the center to pursue Alexander's troops. This created a fatal gap in the Persian line, which Alexander had been waiting for. Leading his Companion Cavalry, he charged at full speed into this gap, aiming straight for Darius.

It was a daring and dangerous move, but that was Alexander's style. He had an uncanny ability to visualize the flow of battle, to see opportunities where others saw only chaos. His daring charge threw the Persian forces into disarray. The sight of their king being targeted caused panic and confusion among the Persian ranks, allowing the Macedonians to press their advantage.

As Darius fled, the battle turned irrevocably in Alexander's favor. His vision, his unorthodox tactics, and his personal courage had won the day. The Battle of Gaugamela was a decisive victory that marked the end of Persian resistance and paved the way for Alexander's unchallenged rule over their empire.

Alexander's strategies at Gaugamela encapsulate his military genius and the power of his visionary leadership. They demonstrate his ability to turn a seemingly impossible situation into a triumph. His vision was not only about grand plans for empire-building or divine associations; it was also about the minute details, the split-second decisions on the battlefield that turned the tide of history.

As we leave the battlefield of Gaugamela, it's worth reflecting on what this victory meant for Alexander's vision. It was not merely a step towards the end of the Persian Empire, but also a validation of Alexander's unconventional tactics and his belief in his own invincibility. The vision that guided him to this monumental victory was the same that had been with him from the beginning: a vision of a world united under his rule, where Greek and Persian, Macedonian and Egyptian could live together in a grand, cosmopolitan empire. In the dust and blood of Gaugamela, that vision was one step closer to becoming a reality.

With the dust of the Gaugamela battlefield still settling, let's turn our focus towards another, perhaps less obvious, aspect of Alexander's exceptional leadership. His mental prowess and his extraordinary ability to inspire his men are qualities that were as integral to his success as his well-documented military strategies. So, sit back and relax as we explore the mental acumen and the inspiring aura of this historical titan.

Alexander was more than just a military leader; he was an inspiring figure who led by example. He shared the hardship of his men, partook in the same food, endured the same harsh weather, and fought on the front lines. These actions were not only strategic but also motivational. His men saw him not as a distant commander, but as one of them, a fellow soldier with the same blood, sweat, and tears.

Alexander's mental prowess played a critical role in his inspiring leadership. His memory was said to be extraordinary. He could call every soldier by name, a fact that greatly increased his men's loyalty and morale. Imagine being a simple foot soldier, fighting thousands of miles away from home, and your king, who commands tens of thousands, knows you by name. It gives a sense of value, a feeling that you're not just a cog in the machine, but an important part of the whole endeavor. This was one of Alexander's many skills that set him apart from other leaders of his time.

Alexander's mental strength was also evident in his ability to remain calm under pressure. He had an almost supernatural ability to think clearly in the heat of battle, making strategic decisions that turned the tide in his favor. This clarity of thought was not the product of chance, but a testament to Alexander's mental discipline and his capacity to keep his emotions in check, traits that he had developed under the tutelage of Aristotle.

But Alexander was not just about discipline and control. He understood the power of passion, of a well-timed speech, of a dramatic gesture. After all, a great leader doesn't just instruct, he inspires. Whether it was a rallying call before the battle, a comforting word to a wounded soldier, or a celebration after a victory, Alexander knew how to kindle the flame of passion in his men's hearts. His words and actions resonated with his men, motivating them to follow him even into the most dangerous battles.

Anecdotes of Alexander's ability to inspire his men abound. One of the most famous is the incident before the battle against the Persians at Issus. His men, worn and nervous, faced a much larger enemy force. Sensing their trepidation, Alexander gathered his men and addressed them. He spoke not of the glory of victory or the spoils of war, but of their shared camaraderie and past victories. His words filled his men with renewed confidence and the courage to face the daunting challenge ahead.

All these instances paint a picture of a leader who was as much a mental giant as he was a military genius. His intellectual prowess, emotional intelligence, and his knack for inspiration were integral parts of his successful leadership. They made him not only a king but also a comrade, a mentor, and a beacon of inspiration for his men.

As we bring this chapter to a close, we see that Alexander's vision was not just a grand design of world conquest. It was also a vision of shared hardship and glory, of leading from the front, of valuing every single person in his army. His vision was a world where a king fought alongside his men, shared their pain, and carried them along in his quest for greatness.

Alexander's military strategies might have won him battles, but it was his mental prowess and his ability to inspire his men that truly built his empire. In the end, it was not the fear of the whip, but the love for their leader, and the belief in his vision, that made his men march thousands of miles, fight countless battles, and create one of the greatest empires the world has ever seen.

ACROSS THE INDUS: THE LIMITS OF VISION

Pour yourself a cup of coffee, tea, or your favorite beverage and settle down for an exciting chapter as we traverse the ancient lands of India with Alexander the Great. A thrilling narrative awaits us, brimming with tales of exotic locales, valiant battles, and the limits of one man's vision.

The year was 326 BC. Alexander, now the uncontested ruler of the vast Persian Empire, set his sights on the lands to the east, the mysterious and culturally rich subcontinent of India. His vision, which had taken him from the sandy beaches of Greece to the Nile Delta, the rugged terrains of Afghanistan, and the scorching deserts of Persia, was now driving him to the verdant and unfamiliar plains of the Punjab.

The expedition to India marked an important point in Alexander's career. His men, war-weary from a decade of continuous campaigning, were a far cry from the enthusiastic force that had left Macedonia. Yet, Alexander, a man driven by an insatiable thirst for knowledge, conquest, and glory, was undeterred by the enormity of the task.

After crossing the daunting peaks of the Hindu Kush, the Macedonian army encountered a completely new world. They marveled at the sight of the mighty Indus River, the lush forests, the exotic animals, and the unique customs and traditions of the people. But with this novel wonderment came the challenges of unfamiliar terrain and unpredictable weather.

The first significant battle in India was at the River Jhelum against King Porus. Despite being heavily outnumbered, Porus and his troops stood their ground, demonstrating the courage and valor that would earn Alexander's admiration. Alexander's strategic prowess was put to a significant test, but ultimately, it was his tactical brilliance and the resilience of his soldiers that led to his victory.

Post the Jhelum encounter, Alexander and his men continued their journey deeper into India. They encountered the Malli tribes who were renowned for their fighting prowess. The struggle against the Malli was fierce, with Alexander, ever the leading-from-the-front commander, sustaining a serious wound. Despite this setback, his indomitable will spurred his men to fight on and eventually subdue the Malli.

But the victorious skirmishes and conquered lands were not enough to sustain the morale of Alexander's troops. They had followed their leader from victory to victory, across the vast expanse of the known world, but their endurance had started to wane. They longed for their homes and families, and the enticing narratives of further eastern conquests no longer held the charm they once did.

These campaigns in India, while rich in encounters and discovery, represented the furthest extent of Alexander's extraordinary vision. Despite his undying spirit, his dream of reaching the "world's end" and the great Ocean—which the Greeks believed encircled the world—were becoming increasingly elusive.

By exploring these campaigns in India, we get a glimpse of Alexander's boundless ambition. We see a man willing to push the envelope, someone who was ready to risk everything in pursuit of his vision. Yet, these accounts also serve as a gentle reminder that even the most ardent visionaries have their limits, that the human element cannot be ignored in the grand scheme of world-conquering plans.

In the next chapter, we will continue exploring Alexander's Indian campaign, with a specific focus on his encounter with King Porus and the consequential decision that marked a turning point in his legendary journey. Stay with us, for the tale of Alexander is as much about the vision as it is about understanding its boundaries.

Welcome back, dear reader! Let's dive back into the rich tapestry of history, where we left Alexander and his troops on the verdant banks of the River Jhelum. Now, we focus on a singular moment of history that not only underscored the grit and valor of the Indian king Porus, but also revealed a side of Alexander often overshadowed by his military genius - his admiration for bravery and honor.

The Battle of the Hydaspes River, modern-day Jhelum, marked the most intense and challenging clash in Alexander's Indian campaign. Here, he faced King Porus, a ruler of the Paurava kingdom in Punjab. In stark contrast to previous battles, Alexander found a formidable adversary in Porus, whose determination and valor gave the Macedonian king a run for his money, quite literally!

The stage for this epic encounter was the Hydaspes River, swollen with monsoon rains. Picture, if you will, a stormy night, the skies echoing the ominous rumble of thunder, the rain lashing relentlessly on Alexander's troops as they made their daring river crossing under the cover of darkness. All this while, Porus had anticipated Alexander's move and was waiting on the opposite bank.

Despite the adverse conditions, Alexander, ever the master strategist, outmaneuvered Porus. He split his forces, leaving part of his army in full view to mislead Porus while he and a chosen band of soldiers crossed the river in the midst of a violent storm.

As dawn broke, the battle began in earnest. Porus' army, though caught off guard, did not falter. The heart of the Indian defense was its war elephants, intimidating creatures that caused havoc among the Macedonian horses. Yet, even this couldn't deter Alexander and his men, who fought with their characteristic determination and tactical ingenuity.

The fight was fierce, and the bravery displayed by both sides was commendable. Yet, it was Porus who stood out in his relentless defiance, even as his men fell around him. His resilience and courage were such that, even in defeat, he won something arguably more enduring than a battle - he won Alexander's deep respect.

In the aftermath of the battle, when Alexander asked Porus how he wished to be treated, the defeated king, still holding onto his royal dignity, replied, "Treat me, O Alexander, like a king." Alexander, impressed by the Indian king's valor and indomitable spirit, not only spared his life but also returned him his kingdom, along with additional lands he had conquered.

This encounter with Porus brought forth a crucial facet of Alexander's character, his respect for valor and courage, regardless of friend or foe. In the epic narrative of Alexander's conquests, it serves as a poignant reminder of the virtues that can shine even in the heart of conflict.

The Battle of the Hydaspes marked the zenith of Alexander's eastward march. Beyond this point, we will see the limits of his vision as his weary troops, yearning for home, refuse to continue further into the unknown eastern lands. But that's a story for our next chapter.

Stay with us, dear reader, as we navigate through the complex character of Alexander the Great. Let us explore how even the most powerful visions have their limits, and how the power of human spirit can manifest in the most unexpected ways, influencing even the greatest of leaders.

Welcome back, dear reader! As we continue to traverse the broad swathes of history with Alexander the Great, we reach a critical junction in his legendary campaign - a moment that starkly reminds us that even the most far-reaching visions have their limits.

Following the victory over King Porus, Alexander's gaze turned farther east, towards the vast and mysterious lands of India that lay beyond the Hydaspes. He dreamed of crossing the Ganges, a river rumoured to be wider and deeper than any he had yet encountered, and of conquering the mighty kingdoms that were said to thrive on its fertile banks. But dreams and reality do not always walk hand in hand.

For eight long years, Alexander's men had marched tirelessly, following their leader's vision across deserts, over mountains, and through rivers. They had fought countless battles, faced untold hardships, and witnessed the unfamiliar cultures and traditions of distant lands. But now, as the mighty Ganges and the formidable Nanda Empire awaited them, they found their resolve faltering.

Alexander, the indomitable leader, the embodiment of the power of vision, stood before his men and spoke of glory, of the unknown Eastern Ocean they were destined to reach, and of the honour that awaited them at the end of their journey. Yet, as he looked at the sea of weary faces before him, he could see their determination wane. The words that had once inspired and invigorated, now fell on exhausted ears.

These men, their bodies scarred by battle, their minds wearied by the endless campaign, longed for the comforts of their homeland. They yearned to return to the familiar landscapes of Macedonia, to their families and loved ones. They had had their fill of glory, of battle, of conquest, and now they sought the simple pleasures of life - peace, stability, and the warmth of home.

The refusal of his army to march further came as a bitter blow to Alexander. It was a painful reminder that the strength of a vision is not solely reliant on its grandeur, or on the charisma of the one who holds it. Instead, its success often hinges on the readiness of those who are expected to follow it.

Faced with mutiny, Alexander was forced to reassess his plans. His dream of marching up to the Eastern Ocean remained just that, a dream. He ordered the construction of a fleet of ships for the journey down the Indus River towards the Southern Ocean, a detour that marked the beginning of his return journey. But even as he did so, he made one final attempt to march eastward, only to turn back again when his men refused.

In this chapter of Alexander's life, we see the stark realization of a visionary leader - that the power of a vision often meets its limits in the endurance of those who bear its weight. It was not a lack of courage or ability that halted Alexander's eastward march, but a deep longing for home among his ranks that he could not quell.

In the grand tapestry of Alexander's life, this moment stands out, not as a failure, but as a testament to the complex interplay of human desires, ambitions, and limitations. It adds depth to our understanding of vision as a powerful yet intricate force that can shape the course of history but remains subject to the very human elements of endurance and longing.

Stay with us, dear reader, as we further unravel the intricate journey of this great leader in our upcoming chapters. A journey filled with conquests, victories, but also loss, and how these experiences shaped the visionary Alexander was. Until then, let's ponder on the fascinating dynamics of vision and the human spirit.

SHADOWS OVER THE VISION

Hello, dear reader, and welcome back! We are about to embark on another critical chapter in Alexander's remarkable life, where we shall bear witness to the physical and mental tolls his unwavering vision and years of incessant campaigning had on him. We'll explore the twilight years of his meteoric journey, years filled with hardship, introspection, and the realization of his mortal limits.

The dream of reaching the Eastern Ocean, the so-called "World's End," had been thwarted, not by the enemy in battle, but by his own weary men longing for home. For the first time, the once invincible Alexander was forced to succumb to a power even he couldn't overcome - the human desire for rest and peace. Yet, despite this setback, Alexander, always the visionary, set his sights on new dreams and ambitions, shifting his course southward towards the Arabian Peninsula. But the Alexander who set foot on this new path was not the same young, energetic king who had embarked on the grand journey eight years prior.

The countless battles, endless marches, and psychological strain of his ambitious campaigns had begun to extract a heavy toll on Alexander. His once robust physique bore the scars of numerous wounds and the stress of continuous warfare. The youthful vigour that had once defined him was slowly giving way to fatigue. His health began to wane, with bouts of fever and illness becoming frequent. Yet, in his characteristic manner, Alexander refused to let these physical setbacks deter him, continuing to push himself and his men towards new conquests.

But the physical strain was not the only shadow looming over Alexander's vision. The mental and emotional toll was arguably even more significant. As the years passed, Alexander found himself increasingly isolated. He was no longer just one among his men, sharing in their toils and hardships. His divinity claims in Egypt and subsequent behaviour had begun to alienate him, creating a chasm between him and his soldiers.

Moreover, the pressure of sustaining the sprawling empire he had built was immense. There were revolts, power struggles, cultural clashes, and administrative challenges that needed his attention, draining him mentally. His ambitious vision of a united empire under one ruler, where Greek and Persian cultures merged, was met with resistance, not only from the conquered but often from his own countrymen, further adding to his emotional burden.

He also grappled with paranoia, perhaps a consequence of his father's assassination and the constant fear of mutiny. He dealt harshly with any perceived threat, resulting in executions of close companions like Philotas and Parmenion, which only added to his growing loneliness and regret.

In these twilight years, Alexander was often caught between his larger-than-life vision and his mortality. He oscillated between his image as a divine conqueror and his reality as a weary man carrying the weight of an empire on his shoulders. He was forced to confront the fragility of his own life and the potential dissolution of his grand dream.

The shadows that loomed over Alexander's vision in his final years were many - physical exhaustion, emotional turmoil, paranoia, and the growing resistance to his vision of cultural fusion. But even as these challenges mounted, Alexander persevered, determined to navigate the labyrinth of complications that his vision had woven around him.

As we conclude this chapter and look towards the next, it is important for us to remember that even the most monumental figures in history, like Alexander, were not immune to human frailties. Their visions, no matter how grand, were tethered to their human form, subjected to the physical and emotional trials of life. In our next chapter, we shall explore another poignant event in Alexander's life – the death of his close friend,

Hephaestion, and its profound impact on him. But for now, let's take a moment to reflect on the resilient spirit of Alexander, who, despite the mounting challenges, never lost sight of his vision.

Welcome back, dear reader! As we journey through the final years of Alexander's incredible life, we now delve into one of the most heart-wrenching episodes in his story, the death of his closest friend and confidant, Hephaestion. The loss of Hephaestion not only had profound personal consequences for Alexander but also serious political implications. So, let's uncover together the deep bonds of friendship that connected these two men and the profound impact of their untimely separation.

From their childhood days in Macedonia, Hephaestion and Alexander had been inseparable. Trained under Aristotle's tutelage, they forged a bond rooted in shared experiences, philosophical discussions, and youthful dreams. They later stood shoulder to shoulder in the heat of battle, and Hephaestion's unwavering loyalty to Alexander became the bedrock of their friendship.

When Hephaestion died suddenly in Ecbatana in 324 BC, reportedly from fever after a banquet, Alexander was shattered. The man who had weathered countless battles, who had built and governed an empire, who had stared death in the face, was brought to his knees by the anguish of personal loss.

He reacted to the news with an outpouring of grief that shocked all who witnessed it. He ordered a period of mourning throughout his empire, cut his hair in sorrow—a traditional Greek mourning practice—and even petitioned the oracle at Siwa to grant Hephaestion divine status.

Beyond the personal loss, Hephaestion's death left a vacuum in Alexander's inner circle. Hephaestion had been not only Alexander's closest friend but also his most trusted advisor. He was the glue that held together the Macedonian aristocracy, a loyalist who eased the tension between Alexander and his other generals. His role was as much political as it was personal. His absence led to a scramble for power among Alexander's remaining companions, further destabilizing an already strained administration.

But more than anything, Hephaestion's death symbolized the end of an era for Alexander. It marked the loss of the last vestige of his youthful days in Macedonia, a time before the weight of his vision and the pressures of his empire had taken a toll on him. With Hephaestion, a part of Alexander's past, his connection to a simpler time, died as well.

This tragedy cast long shadows over Alexander's vision. His dreams of further conquests and cultural unification took a backseat as he grappled with the enormity of his personal loss. His actions post-Hephaestion's death, such as the overly extravagant funeral games and his severe grieving, demonstrated a king struggling with loss and loneliness, a man coming to terms with his own mortality.

The death of Hephaestion served as a poignant reminder of the fragility of human life, even for a man as extraordinary as Alexander. In a strange way, it grounded him, brought him face-to-face with the reality of life's impermanence—a concept that must have seemed alien to a man who had, for a decade, appeared invincible.

As we continue our journey into the final years of Alexander's life, we will see how this personal loss and the emotional turmoil that ensued further influenced his actions and decisions, how the visionary leader coped with the loss of his friend, his confidant, and his anchor. But that's a tale for another chapter. Until then, dear reader, let's remember the undying bond of friendship that connected Alexander and Hephaestion—a bond so powerful that it continues to echo through the annals of history.

Hello again, dear reader! As we continue to explore the twilight years of Alexander's life, we now focus on his grandiose plans for further conquests and cultural unification. Even as the shadows of personal loss and physical decline began to darken his life, Alexander's indomitable spirit remained unquenched. His visionary zeal shone through, and despite the mounting challenges, his mind teemed with ambitious projects.

The extent of Alexander's imperial vision was truly astounding. Even after a decade of continuous conquests, his ambition was not sated. He intended to push the boundaries of his empire even further, to places his army dreaded to march. The lands towards the west, including Arabia and even the unexplored territories of the Mediterranean, beckoned him.

Arabia fascinated Alexander with its wealth of incense and spices, a key trade component that could strengthen his empire's economic prowess. He intended to conquer it, not merely for its resources but also as a strategic step towards becoming the unrivaled master of the Mediterranean. According to his plan, an Arabian conquest would provide a base for further westward expansion, possibly reaching as far as the pillars of Hercules, modern-day Gibraltar.

However, Alexander's plans extended beyond military conquests. He envisioned a grand cultural unification, blending the best of Greek and Eastern traditions. He encouraged intermarriages between his Greek soldiers and Persian women, himself setting the precedent by marrying Roxana, a Sogdian princess, and later Stateira II and Parysatis II, daughters of the Persian King Darius III.

He incorporated Persians into his army, employed them in administrative roles, and even adopted Persian court practices. He dreamt of an empire where Greek thought and philosophy would mix with the rich traditions of the East, giving rise to a culture that was greater than the sum of its parts. These moves, however, were met with resistance from his Macedonian comrades, who viewed them as a betrayal of their Hellenic culture.

Alexander, in his visionary fervor, was undeterred. He believed this amalgamation was essential for the long-term stability of his vast empire. He understood that his territories were too diverse and too large to be ruled effectively under a strictly Hellenic system. The cultural unification he sought was a daring experiment in governance and societal integration, a testament to his forward-thinking approach.

And yet, as grand as Alexander's plans were, they were destined to remain unfulfilled. His untimely death meant many of his ambitions were left unrealized. His dreams of further conquests and a harmonious, unified empire passed away with him. His death, however, was not the end of his story. His successors, the Diadochi, and the empires they would establish carried echoes of Alexander's grand vision. But we will explore these intriguing chapters of history in subsequent sections.

In the next chapter, we shall examine the immediate aftermath of Alexander's sudden death and the legacy of his vision. As we continue our journey through Alexander's life, we find that even as the shadows gathered around him, his vision of a unified empire under his rule remained the defining aspect of his life. Until then, dear reader, let us marvel at the unyielding spirit of this extraordinary leader, his dreams undimmed even in the face of adversity.

THE LEGACY OF A VISION

Greetings again, dear reader. We continue our journey through the life of Alexander, arriving now at an unexpected and pivotal point – his untimely and sudden death. While Alexander's life was characterized by swift action and relentless movement, his abrupt demise brought a new dynamic within his empire.

The year was 323 BC. Alexander, who had returned to Babylon after his exhausting Indian campaign, fell severely ill. The man who had led his troops through some of the harshest terrains, fought in frontlines, and had survived deadly battles, succumbed to an illness. As the news of Alexander's death spread, it was met with disbelief. It seemed impossible that the great conqueror, the invincible warrior, was no more.

The immediate reaction of his empire was one of shock and uncertainty. Alexander had always been the unifying figure, the driving force that held his vast empire together. His charismatic leadership was the glue that bonded diverse cultures, people, and regions into one grand entity. His sudden absence created a power vacuum that destabilized his empire.

Alexander's death marked the beginning of the "Successor" period in which his top generals, known as the Diadochi, began to vie for control of different parts of the empire. His premature death had left no undisputed heir or a succession plan in place, resulting in a power struggle that would last for decades.

The Macedonian army, loyal to Alexander till their last breath, was bereft and leaderless. They found it hard to imagine serving anyone other than Alexander. They had marched thousands of miles, fought numerous battles, not for the glory of Macedonia or even for their own glory, but for Alexander. His vision had been their guiding force, and his death left them adrift.

The civilians within his empire, from Greece to Egypt and Persia, reacted with a mix of anxiety, relief, and curiosity. For some, Alexander was a liberator who freed them from the yoke of tyranny; for others, he was an invader who disrupted their way of life. Regardless, his death signaled an end of an era and the beginning of an uncertain future.

In the cities he founded, particularly Alexandria in Egypt, the news of his death was met with profound sorrow. Here, Alexander was not just a conqueror, but a visionary leader who had transformed their cities into centers of learning and culture. His death was mourned as the loss of a great benefactor.

As we delve deeper into the reaction of his empire, we realize that Alexander's death was not just the end of a monarch; it was the loss of a vision, a dream that spanned across cultures and continents. A dream of a unified world under one rule, a dream that was as grand as it was audacious.

As we turn the page to the next chapter, we'll explore the aftermath of Alexander's death in greater detail. We'll witness the division of his empire among his generals and the impact his visionary leadership had on the world, even in his absence. The story of Alexander does not end with his death. If anything, it becomes even more intriguing. Join me, dear reader, as we continue to unravel the legacy of Alexander the Great.

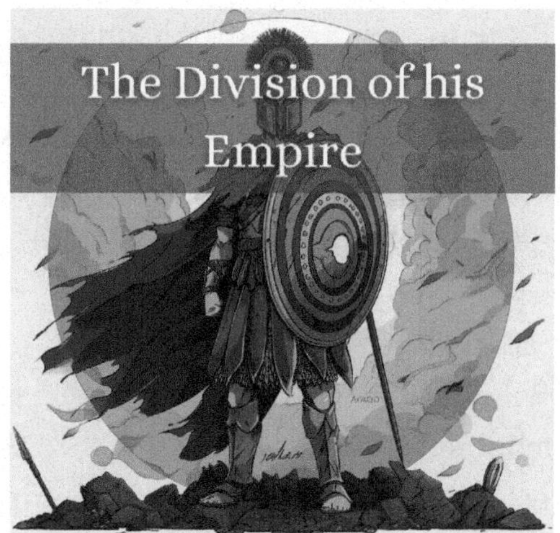

Hello again, dear reader. As we continue our exploration of the world after Alexander, we find ourselves amidst the chaos and power struggles that ensued in the aftermath of his sudden death. The expansive empire, held together by Alexander's unifying vision and strong hand, now faced an uncertain future. Today, we explore how the absence of an undisputed heir led to the division of his empire among his generals.

To understand this complex period, we need to familiarize ourselves with Alexander's most trusted generals, the Diadochi, which literally means "successors". These were men who had marched side by side with Alexander, shared his trials and triumphs, and were his closest confidants. Among these were figures like Ptolemy, Seleucus, Perdiccas, and Antigonus, each of whom played a significant role in shaping the post-Alexander era.

In the initial days following Alexander's death, Perdiccas, who held the office of the chiliarch (a role similar to a vizier), was considered as a regent. Roxana, Alexander's wife, was pregnant and Perdiccas assumed the responsibility of the empire, intending to protect it for Alexander's unborn child. However, his rule was rife with conflicts and internal strife.

Ptolemy, another of Alexander's experienced generals, took control of Egypt, making it a center of wealth and knowledge, and establishing the Ptolemaic dynasty. Notably, he was also responsible for transferring Alexander's body to Alexandria, a decision that further solidified his claim to power.

Meanwhile, Seleucus, initially appointed as the satrap of Babylon by Perdiccas, managed to secure vast territories that spanned from modern-day Turkey to India, eventually establishing the Seleucid Empire. His dominion marked a significant impact on the cultural and political landscapes of the Middle East.

On the other hand, Antigonus, an ambitious and seasoned general, aimed for overall control and waged war against his fellow successors. These wars, known as the Wars of the Diadochi, resulted in changing alliances and a significant reshaping of Alexander's empire.

As we step back and view this series of events, it's clear that the unity and vision that Alexander brought to his empire began to crumble with his absence. Each of the Diadochi had their own vision and understanding of how the empire should be ruled, influenced by their personal ambitions, cultural backgrounds, and experiences under Alexander's leadership.

However, it's crucial to note that despite the division, the Diadochi did maintain some key elements of Alexander's empire. Greek culture and language continued to flourish in these regions, an aspect we'll delve deeper into in our next segment.

The division of Alexander's empire is a testament to his extraordinary leadership. It took multiple successors, each controlling different territories, to manage the vast lands that Alexander once ruled single-handedly. This period of history serves as a powerful reminder of Alexander's exceptional ability to unify diverse cultures and regions under his singular vision.

Next, we shall take a closer look at how, despite the divisions, Alexander's vision managed to resonate through centuries, marking an era known as the Hellenistic period. Please continue to journey with me, dear reader, as we unveil the lasting impact of Alexander's visionary leadership.

Welcome back, dear reader. We have journeyed through wars, power shifts, and political maneuvers that followed Alexander's death. We've witnessed the division of his empire among his generals, each asserting control over vast territories. Today, we delve deeper into a fascinating aspect of Alexander's legacy - the spread of Hellenism and the lasting impact of his visions.

In simple terms, Hellenism is the adoption and spread of Greek culture, and this process was dramatically accelerated during and after Alexander's reign. Despite the division of his empire, Alexander's vision of a unified cultural and political landscape significantly impacted the regions he conquered, leading to a broad dissemination of Greek ideas, traditions, and language.

Under Alexander's influence, Greek became the lingua franca, the common language across the empire, from the eastern Mediterranean to parts of Asia and Africa. This universal language facilitated trade and communication, aiding in the exchange of ideas and fostering a sense of unity among diverse cultures.

The cities founded by Alexander, especially Alexandria in Egypt, became melting pots of various cultures. Here, Greek architecture and thought blended seamlessly with local traditions, resulting in a unique and rich cultural fabric. These cosmopolitan cities attracted scholars, artists, and thinkers, becoming significant centers of learning and culture.

In the realm of art, the Hellenistic period saw the emergence of new styles and techniques. Influences from the East were fused with Greek artistic traditions, leading to more expressive and dramatic artworks. The famous statue of Laocoön and His Sons, which depicts a Trojan priest and his sons in a moment of tragic struggle, is a prime example of Hellenistic art's emotional intensity and dynamism.

Moreover, Greek philosophical schools, such as Stoicism and Epicureanism, also gained prominence during this period. These schools of thought, with their emphasis on ethics and individual happiness, deeply influenced societies far beyond Greece and continue to resonate with people today.

In the scientific domain, the Hellenistic period was a time of significant advancements. The establishment of the Library of Alexandria by Ptolemy I, one of Alexander's generals, led to remarkable developments in various fields, including mathematics, astronomy, and medicine. Great minds like Euclid, Archimedes, and Eratosthenes thrived in this intellectually stimulating environment.

While Alexander might not have foreseen the exact outcomes of Hellenism, his vision for a united empire where diverse cultures learned from each other significantly facilitated this cultural exchange. His openness to adopting foreign cultures, languages, and customs, as we've discussed in previous chapters, was a testament to his progressive vision.

Through Hellenism, Alexander's influence extended far beyond his lifetime. His visions of unity and cultural fusion have left an indelible imprint on history, shaping our world in ways that are still visible today. As we delve further into the impact of Alexander's visionary leadership, let's remember that even in the face of division and conflict, his legacy continued to resonate, forever altering the course of human history.

In the next chapter, we revisit Alexander's vision, analyzing its power and its juxtaposition with his human flaws. As we approach the final sections of our book, we hope you continue to enjoy this historical journey, shedding light on the extraordinary life and enduring legacy of Alexander the Great.

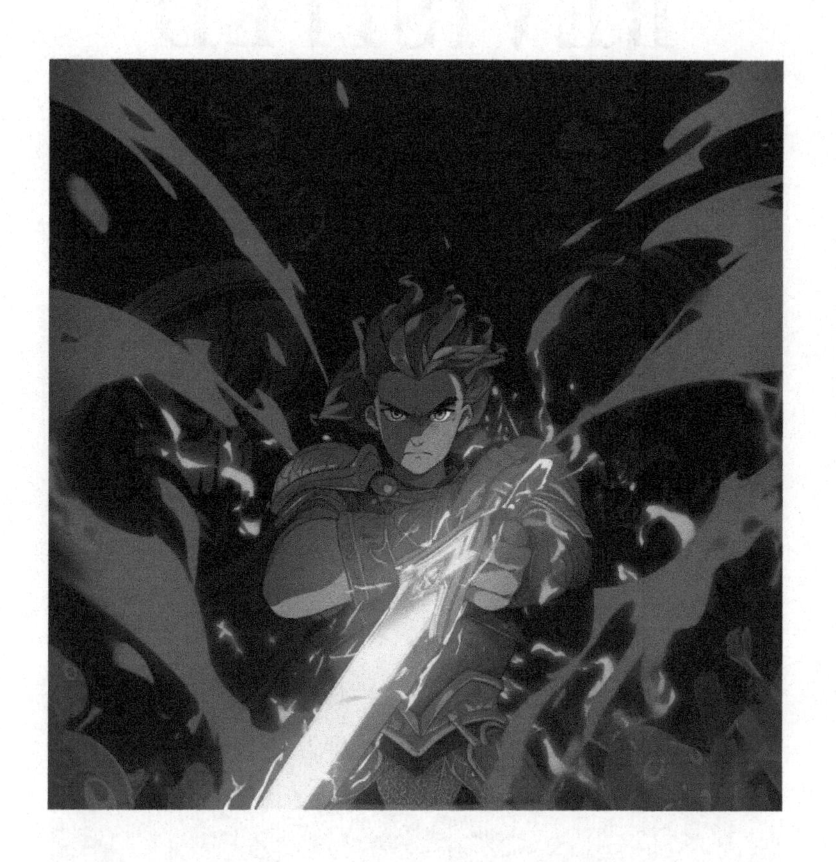

THE VISION REVISITED

Hello again, dear reader, as we continue our journey into the life and legacy of Alexander the Great. We've navigated the tumultuous waters of his early years, witnessed the evolution of his vision, and traced the aftermath of his death. Now, it's time to revisit and analyze the power of Alexander's vision in a broader context.

Remember, a vision, in essence, is not merely a future projection. It's a magnetic force, a guiding light that leads, influences, and shapes both actions and outcomes. Alexander's vision was no different. It was a powerful catalyst that drove him and his vast empire towards a shared goal.

From an early age, Alexander possessed a vision of an expansive Greek Empire, unified and powerful. Despite the grandeur of this vision, what made it truly powerful was Alexander's unwavering commitment to it. He was not merely a dreamer, but a man of action. His visions were not confined to the realm of ideas but were translated into tangible actions that ultimately sculpted the contours of the world as we know it today.

Alexander's vision was not just for conquest, but for the integration of cultures and creation of a harmonious empire where the wisdom of the East and West could merge. His encouragement of marriages between his soldiers and foreign women, his own marriage to Roxana of Bactria, and his adoption of Persian customs and dress, all testify to this grand vision.

However, Alexander's vision was also characterized by an insatiable ambition. His aim to establish a universal empire and his belief in his divine role made him unstoppable. The great Battle of Gaugamela, where he was outnumbered, yet emerged victorious, stands testament to the strength of his vision. He could see beyond the immediate, and his strategic acumen transformed perceived obstacles into stepping stones towards his dream.

His vision extended to the administrative sphere as well. Unlike many conquerors who simply pillaged and moved on, Alexander established many cities, most notably Alexandria, spreading Greek culture and political systems. The institutions he set up, based on merit rather than birth, and the cultural syncretism he encouraged, were revolutionary for the time.

It's also essential to note the inspiring aspect of Alexander's vision. He had the unique ability to instill his vision into the hearts and minds of his soldiers, who followed him through deserts, across mountains, and into countless battles. His charisma and personal valor on the battlefield, his demonstration of shared hardship and rewards, fostered intense loyalty among his men, fueling their drive to realize his vision.

In revisiting Alexander's vision, we understand that it was not static but an evolving entity that adapted based on his experiences and the changing landscapes of the vast territories he conquered. This flexibility and openness to incorporate new elements into his vision made it resilient and potent.

In essence, the power of Alexander's vision lay in its expansiveness, its blend of ambition and pragmatism, its inspiring nature, and its adaptability. It was a vision that was both a projection of a desired future and a robust tool to navigate the complexities of the present.

As we delve deeper into this final chapter, we will juxtapose Alexander's visionary prowess with his human flaws, adding another layer of complexity to our understanding of this remarkable figure. So, dear reader, let's proceed to peel away the layers of this enigmatic leader's life and legacy.

chapter 26

Welcome back, dear reader, as we continue to revisit Alexander's vision and delve into the complex fabric of his character. In the previous sections, we've lauded his vision, praised his foresight, and admired his fortitude. Yet, we would do a disservice to the memory of Alexander and the lessons his life can teach us if we were to ignore his human flaws. The full picture of Alexander, much like any person, lies in the juxtaposition of his visionary prowess and his human weaknesses.

You see, the same vision that led to the spreading of Hellenistic culture, that brought forth an era of knowledge and blending of traditions, was also the vision that fueled wars, led to the loss of thousands of lives, and sometimes revealed a side of Alexander that was far from virtuous.

Alexander was driven by an insatiable ambition, a hunger for conquest and glory that knew no bounds. His vision, grand as it was, often pushed him to wage relentless war, showing little regard for the peace and stability of the territories he ruled. His campaigns were marked by instances of extreme violence, such as the brutal sack of Tyre and the torching of Persepolis, showing that the great visionary was also capable of great cruelty.

Alexander's sense of invincibility and his belief in his divine mission to conquer the world sometimes bordered on the delusional. It was a belief that made him disregard the advice of his counselors and even dismiss the well-being of his soldiers. This is best exemplified in the Indian campaign, where his troops, exhausted and far from home, were pushed to their limits.

His autocratic tendencies and quick temper also presented another side of his character. Alexander demanded absolute loyalty from his men, and those who crossed him often met with a swift end, as the case of Cleitus the Black illustrates. Alexander killed Cleitus, his old friend and comrade, in a fit of rage, displaying a volatile personality that could override his typically strategic mindset.

Yet, it's essential to view these flaws not as isolated character defects but as an integral part of the complex personality that was Alexander the Great. His flaws were inseparable from his strengths. His ambition, while leading to violence and conquest, was also the driving force behind his grand vision of unity and cultural amalgamation. His autocratic style and swift decision-making, though it cost him personal relationships, were also vital in maintaining the efficiency and discipline of his vast empire.

In studying Alexander, we must strive to understand the man in his entirety, acknowledging both his visionary leadership and his human flaws. Only then can we fully appreciate his impact on history and the valuable lessons his life provides.

As we progress further into this chapter, we will be delving into Alexander's role in shaping the world as a visionary leader. It's a journey that takes us to the heart of his life and legacy, and I invite you to join me as we continue to uncover the layers of this fascinating historical figure.

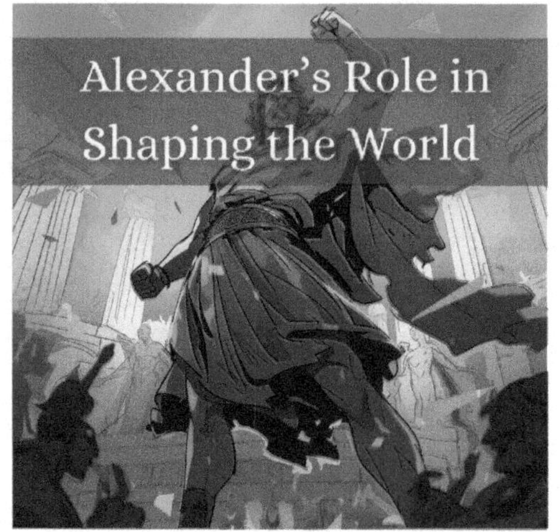

As we have traced the steps of Alexander the Great across continents, one theme echoes through each chapter: Alexander's exceptional ability to envision the world not as it was, but as it could be. Through this final examination of Alexander's role in shaping the world as a visionary leader, we aim to understand the magnitude of his legacy, defined by his unique blend of tactical genius, diplomatic prowess, and cultural sensitivity.

Alexander's vision was unique in its universalism. Unlike many rulers of his time, Alexander sought not merely to conquer, but also to unify. The ambition to unite vast and diverse territories under one banner might be viewed as a pipe dream by some, yet for Alexander, it was a plausible goal that he doggedly pursued. His vision extended beyond the immediacy of military victory, foreseeing a world empire that melded together cultures, languages, and traditions.

This blend of cultures, known as Hellenism, marked a significant departure from the prevailing practice of maintaining cultural distinctions between conquerors and the conquered. Alexander encouraged marriages between his Greek soldiers and foreign women, personally leading by example when he wed Roxana of Bactria. He adopted foreign customs and attire, much to the chagrin of some of his traditional Macedonian companions. Yet in doing so, he demonstrated a level of cultural respect and understanding that was far beyond his time.

Alexander's leadership style is an exemplar of what is now known as 'transformational leadership'. He motivated his followers to work towards a common goal that transcended their personal interests. The inspiring vision that he presented, coupled with his charismatic personality, spurred his men to follow him to the ends of the known world and beyond.

Alexander also understood the power of symbolism and image. He often placed himself in the heat of battle, an act that, while dangerous, bolstered his image as a courageous leader who shared the risks with his men. His belief in his divine destiny, reinforced by his visit to the Oracle of Ammon, created an aura around him that deeply impressed both his friends and enemies.

However, it's essential to remember that Alexander's vision, while extraordinary, was not without its limitations. As we've explored, his relentless ambition, his temper, and his occasional inability to accept counsel also defined his leadership style. These human flaws sometimes undermined his visionary goals and, in some instances, led to unnecessary conflicts and hardships.

But, in the grand scope of history, the power of Alexander's vision, his unique leadership style, and his enduring legacy far outweigh his shortcomings. He didn't just conquer lands and cities, but also minds and hearts, fostering an environment that encouraged cultural exchange and mutual respect. His empire, though short-lived, left an indelible mark on the world.

Even two millennia after his death, we still look back on Alexander as an iconic figure - a visionary leader whose grand dream reshaped the world. As we conclude this chapter, it becomes evident that Alexander's true greatness lay not in his undefeated military campaign but in his daring vision of a united world. The man may have been flawed, but the vision - the vision was truly extraordinary.

CONCLUSION

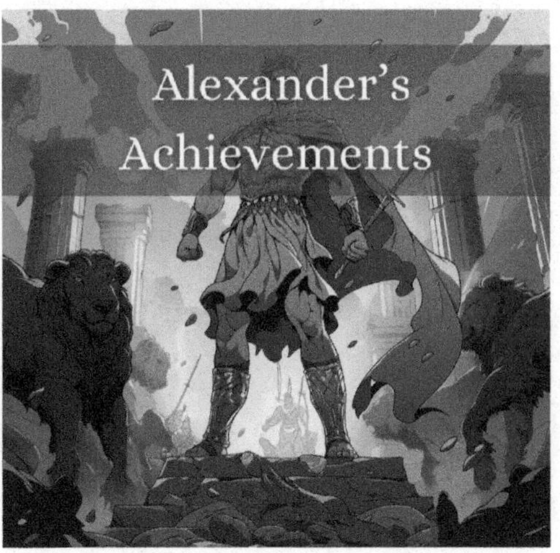

As we have reached the end of our exploration of Alexander the Great's life, it's worth taking a step back to encapsulate the magnitude of his achievements and the extraordinary vision that guided him. This journey has taken us from his early life in Macedonia to his final days in Babylon, providing us a holistic perspective of the man, the warrior, the visionary, and the leader.

In just over a decade, Alexander managed to expand his dominion from the small kingdom of Macedonia to an empire that stretched from Greece to Egypt and as far east as India. His military successes were undoubtedly a testament to his strategic brilliance, courage, and unwavering ambition. Each battle, from the swift victory at Granicus to the pivotal confrontation at Gaugamela and the fierce combat in the dense forests of India, reflects Alexander's adaptability and his innovative tactics that consistently outmaneuvered his opponents.

However, as we have emphasized throughout this book, Alexander's legacy extends beyond his military conquests. His true genius, arguably, lay in his ability to envision a world united under a single banner, embracing a fusion of cultures and traditions. This vision was radical and unprecedented, and Alexander pursued it with an unyielding determination.

Alexander's deep respect for various cultures was an integral part of his vision. His policy of cultural assimilation, manifested in his personal adoption of foreign customs and encouraging intermarriage between his soldiers and local populations, showed his commitment to creating a harmonious empire rather than a patchwork of subjugated territories.

He dared to dream of an empire where Greek thought and local traditions would cross-fertilize, leading to the emergence of a unique culture – a vision that gave birth to Hellenism. His dream did bear fruit, even though it was after his demise, marking the Hellenistic period as one of the most culturally vibrant epochs in history.

His attributes as a visionary leader shone through his ability to inspire his men, his strategic foresight, and his willingness to break with tradition when it served his larger goal. Alexander's charisma was an undeniable factor in his success, capturing the loyalty of his troops and the admiration, or perhaps awe, of those he conquered.

However, our examination would be incomplete without acknowledging Alexander's flaws. His unchecked ambition, his volatile temper, and his resistance to accepting counsel from his advisors often led to unwanted conflicts and pushed him to the brink of overreaching his capabilities.

Nevertheless, when we summarize Alexander's achievements and his visionary attributes, his remarkable qualities distinctly outweigh his imperfections. In the pantheon of history's greatest figures, Alexander stands out not just as a victorious military leader but, more importantly, as a visionary with the power to alter the course of history. His vision, a united world where diverse cultures coexist and enrich each other, was indeed far ahead of his time.

While the man known as Alexander the Great left the world stage more than two millennia ago, his vision and his legacy continue to fascinate and inspire us. It is this enduring influence that truly cements Alexander's place in history as one of the most visionary leaders the world has ever known. The world, as Alexander saw it, was not a series of barriers and divisions, but a vast tapestry of potential unity and shared understanding - a vision as relevant today as it was over two thousand years ago.

Throughout our exploration of Alexander the Great's life and legacy, we have been captivated by his immense military prowess, his bold ambition, and his boundary-defying vision. However, beyond understanding his achievements in his time, it is equally crucial to gauge the influence of his vision on subsequent world history and leadership.

Alexander's vision was monumental, far-reaching, and profoundly transformative. It reached beyond the immediacy of battles and conquests, steering towards the creation of a unified world where diverse cultures could coexist and intermingle freely. The influence of this vision, which arguably set the foundation for globalization centuries before the term even existed, can be traced throughout the annals of world history.

The empire that Alexander built did not survive long after his death. His untimely demise led to the fragmentation of his vast territory among his generals, known as the Diadochi, culminating in the Hellenistic kingdoms. However, this dispersion did not diminish the influence of his vision but rather amplified it. The wide-spread Hellenistic culture across these kingdoms served as a vibrant testament to Alexander's dream of cultural amalgamation. This period saw an extraordinary cross-pollination of Greek philosophy, Middle-Eastern traditions, and Eastern thought, marking a golden era of scientific and artistic advancements. The philosophies of Stoicism and Epicureanism, the advancements in mathematics by Euclid, and the astronomical insights by Aristarchus and Hipparchus are some of the hallmarks of this era.

Moreover, the political framework of Alexander's empire, characterized by a single authority with widespread regional powers, arguably laid the groundwork for future empires, including the Roman and Byzantine. His unique leadership style, a blend of charisma, courage, strategic brilliance, and visionary foresight, has been analyzed, admired, and often emulated by leaders across centuries.

Alexander's vision of a united world still resonates strongly in the modern concept of global citizenship. His legacy serves as a potent reminder that humanity shares more commonalities than differences, a thought that is even more vital in today's interconnected world. The international exchange of ideas, cultural fusion, and mutual respect for diverse traditions that Alexander envisioned are the cornerstones of our global society today.

Moreover, Alexander's approach to leadership - inspiring loyalty, leading from the front, valuing diverse insights, and adapting swiftly to changing situations - are principles that remain relevant to effective leadership. From boardrooms to political platforms, leaders worldwide draw lessons from Alexander's strategic foresight, his ability to inspire, and his determination to pursue a vision, regardless of the challenges that lay in his path.

The saga of Alexander the Great, therefore, is not confined to the past. It is a living narrative, an ongoing influence that shapes our understanding of leadership and our approach to cultural diversity. Alexander's vision, transcending the constraints of his time, continues to echo in our collective consciousness, encouraging us to look beyond borders and differences towards a more inclusive, interconnected world. It serves as a timeless testament to the power of a compelling vision in shaping history and influencing generations.

As we close this exploration, let's reflect on this enduring legacy of Alexander the Great, a legacy that prompts us to dream, to question, to innovate, and above all, to envision a world that thrives on unity in diversity, just as he did more than two thousand years ago. His vision was not just his path to greatness; it is his most enduring contribution to the world, as powerful today as it was in the era of Alexander the Great.

EPILOGUE

As we reach the end of our journey through Alexander the Great's life and legacy, it's important to contemplate the contemporary relevance of his visionary leadership. Can a leader from more than two thousand years ago still offer lessons applicable to our 21st-century world? The answer, as we shall see, is a resounding 'yes'.

Even today, Alexander's leadership approach stands as a blueprint for how one can inspire and lead effectively. His ability to galvanize a diverse group of individuals towards a common goal, his instinctive knack for strategy, his penchant for leading from the front, all underline essential qualities for contemporary leadership. His vision, built on the pillars of unity in diversity and cultural exchange, is remarkably pertinent in today's interconnected world.

Alexander's leadership was not confined to commanding his army but extended to his vision of integrating the conquered peoples into his empire. Today's world is filled with diverse workforces. Leaders, more than ever, need to be able to navigate cultural differences, leverage the diversity of thoughts and ideas, and create inclusive environments where everyone feels valued, just as Alexander did.

Furthermore, the fusion of cultures Alexander promoted serves as an early form of globalization. In our world, defined by the rapid exchange of information, cultures, and ideas across borders, his vision for a blended, inclusive world feels prophetic. His rule and subsequent spread of Hellenistic culture represent a seminal moment in human history, when the insular societies of ancient times began opening up to each other's ideas and innovations. Today, we live that vision, albeit in a digital space.

But as much as we can learn from Alexander's successes, we must also acknowledge his failures. His intoxication with power, his incapability to handle dissent, and his sometimes impulsive decisions remind us that even great leaders can falter when they lose sight of their original vision and let their personal desires take precedence.

Another key lesson we can extract from Alexander's life is the importance of succession planning. His unexpected death led to chaos and fragmentation of the vast empire he had built. This underlines the necessity for today's leaders to ensure their vision is institutionalized, capable of enduring beyond their tenure. They must nurture future leaders who can carry forward the vision and ensure its realization.

In conclusion, while the world of Alexander the Great might seem remote and distinct from ours, the core principles of his leadership and vision are timeless. They endure, crossing the boundaries of time and geography, to find relevance in our age of digital information and global interaction. Whether it's managing diverse teams, integrating cultures, or planning for the future, we find that the lessons from Alexander's visionary leadership remain as instructive as ever.

The true power of Alexander's vision lies not just in the past, but in its ability to influence the present and guide the future. As we step into an era of unprecedented change and challenges, we can look back at Alexander the Great, draw from his strengths, learn from his weaknesses, and hopefully, steer our course towards a world as united and forward-looking as he had envisioned.

And so, even as we close the book, the story of Alexander's visionary leadership continues to unfold, teaching, inspiring, and challenging us to become better leaders, better visionaries, and better global citizens.

We have travelled a long way, tracing the path of Alexander the Great, a man whose life's journey began more than 2,300 years ago. We delved into the intricacies of his visions, witnessed his successes, understood his failures, and discerned the lessons his life offers. Now, as we reach the end, it's time to collect our thoughts and reflect on the essence of this extraordinary journey.

Alexander was not just a historical figure. He was a visionary who dared to dream big, to dream beyond the conventional limits of his time. His ambitions were not confined to his homeland of Macedonia but encompassed the vast, unknown world beyond. He was driven by a powerful vision of unity and cultural assimilation that, in many ways, was millennia ahead of its time.

Yet, in Alexander, we also see the unmistakable human traits that made him real and relatable. His passions, his aspirations, his joys, and his sorrows. His life was not just a tale of relentless conquests but a human story, where he experienced friendship, love, grief, and despair. He, like us, was a human being navigating the challenges of life, albeit on a far grander scale.

This book set out to explore the power of Alexander's vision. And what we discovered was a multifaceted power that went beyond military strategy and territorial conquest. His vision was transformative, helping to shape the world by spreading Hellenistic culture far and wide, fostering unprecedented levels of cross-cultural interaction, and laying the groundwork for the future course of Western civilization. His influence can still be felt today, in the global, interconnected, and diverse world that we live in.

However, as we ponder on his legacy, we must not overlook the flaws and failures that beset Alexander. His story serves as a reminder that vision, without the balance of wisdom, can lead to overreach and disaster. His impulsive decisions, driven by personal ambition and pride, often led to tragic consequences. And his disregard for succession planning ultimately resulted in the disintegration of his vast empire.

These lessons from Alexander's life and vision hold significant relevance for us today. As we navigate the complexities of our modern world, we can draw inspiration from his ability to envision a united world, learn from his strategic acumen, and derive caution from his overreaches and missteps.

Finally, this exploration of Alexander's life has not just been a historical investigation. It has been a study in human potential, in the power of vision, and in the profound impact one individual can have on the course of history. Alexander's story teaches us that while our time on this earth is limited, the power of a compelling vision is not. It can transcend time, survive the ages, and continue to influence generations to come.

As we close this book, let us carry forward the insights gleaned from Alexander's journey. For while we have reached the end of his tale, the power of his vision and the lessons it imparts remain, continuing to illuminate our path and enrich our understanding of what it truly means to be a visionary leader.

Made in the USA
Las Vegas, NV
05 August 2023